#FAITHGOALS

Copyright © 2019 by Sharonda Johnson.

All rights reserved. Printed in the United States of America. No part of this book may be used or reproduced in any manner whatsoever without written permission except in the case of brief quotations em- bodied in critical articles or reviews.

For information contact :
PO BOX 4121, Fredericksburg, VA 22402
http://www.sharondaarlise.home.blog

Book and Cover design by Sharonda Johnson
ISBN: 9781075222566

First Edition: August, 2019

THERE IS SO MUCH POWER IN PRAYER.
It is my prayer that this journal will be a helpful tool to grow closer in your journey of spending time with God for both new and mature believers.

Siena,
I pray this book is a tool to strengthen your walk w/ the Lord.
♡ Sharonda

love
Sharonda

#FAITH GOALS

About the Author

MY MISSION IS TO HELP HEAL, EMPOWER + ENCOURAGE WOMEN AND GIRLS ALL OVER THE WORLD TO GROW THEIR RELATIONSHIP WITH GOD.

Hi! I am Sharonda Johnson. I take so much pleasure in being of service to others by spreading the love of Jesus. In fact, My passions are fulfilled through being the hands + feet of Jesus. My calling and purpose is helping people to live in freedom, despite their past and current challenges.

I enjoy serving the community through my local church, international missions, and spreading the love of God in each encounter I have with others. It is important to me that others feel the love and power of God.

www.sharondaarlise.home.blog

What is prayer?

- Prayer is simply talking to God.

- Prayer is having access to the creator of the world, and having a line of open communication with Him.

- Prayer is opening yourself up to listening to the God who created all, oversees all, and breathes life into every living creature.

- I've learned not to trust my heart always to have the desire to seek God. In other words take every opportunity to pray when you don't feel like it.

Ephesians 6:18 says, "And pray in the Spirit on all occasions with all kinds of prayers and requests"— for it is only the work of the Holy Spirit that enables us to pray as we ought.

How to use prayer prompt pages

I've included Prayer Prompt Pages to help you develop a prayer habit. There are pages titled with a question and a scripture as a guide. These prayer prompts are meant to inspire you and give you options when praying.

The best thing about the Prayer Prompt Pages in this book is that they serve as a guide but you get to choose how you want to talk to God in your own unique way.

Please take every opportunity to make them your own!

There is no right or wrong way to use them, they are included as an added resource.

Pray Out Loud

TIPS TO GET PAST THE FEAR OF PRAYING OUT LOUD.

- Its okay to start off with short prayers. Long prayers aren't more valuable to God than short prayers.
- Focus on the reason why you are praying for example pray by thanking God or pray for your needs. The most important part is you are praying to God who loves you.
- Take a deep breath and invite the Holy Spirit to speak. Be unafraid to follow him as he leads you. Silently pray "Come Holy Spirit" and invite him to give you the right words.
- Comparison is the thief of joy, so Be Authentic. Pray in your own style. It doesn't have to sound a certain way, or like anyone else.
- Remember God created you. He loves you and he wants to hear you just as much as he wants to hear anyone else. He's after your heart when you pray alone or if you are praying with others.
- The more you pray out loud the easier it becomes. So just keep praying.

Tips to pray on days you don't feel like it

Sit in silence
Just say Jesus
Read the Psalms
Write a letter to God
Make a gratitude list
Pray for someone else
Pray your life scripture out loud
Read over past journal entries
Ask a someone else to pray for you
Search inspirational prayers

Things to remember about God when you pray

God is all-powerful.
God is all-knowing.
God has a good plan for your life.
God loves you completely.
God is fully capable of meeting each and every need you have ... He often just does it in ways you don't expect.
God is fully capable in dealing with our stinking attitudes

How to use scripture affirmations

Scripture can be a great way to "affirm" yourself and to remember what God says about you. Its a great place to start by using your favorite verses to help put your thoughts into the right perspective.

Here are some examples:

-I am a child of God. John 1:12
-I am God's masterpiece. Ephesians 2:10
-I do not fear because God strengthens me. Isaiah 41:10
-I am full with the joy of the Lord. Isaiah 42:10
-Through prayer, the peace of God guards my heart & mind. Philippians 4:7

While using this book to grow take some time to write down some affirmations that you can use in your daily life.

THE SECRET IS
SIMPLE PRAY ON
YOUR BEST DAYS

+

PRAY ON YOUR
WORST DAYS

But Jesus himself would often slip away to the wilderness and pray.
—Luke 5:16, AMP

The Enemy's Tactics

Deception +Lies:
Satan is a deceiver. He is a liar. From the very first time he entered the scene he started off by deceiving Eve. He caused her to doubt what God had said to her. Satan will attempt to deceive you into believing in him instead of what God says in his Word. Are you believing lies instead of truth today about who God says you are? Are you stuck in a place of doubt?

Condemnation:
Perhaps you cannot seem to escape the feeling of shame and condemnation over your past. The Lord says that you are a new creation in Christ and that all things are new. If you are having thoughts of condemnation and feeling like you are unloved by God then you are under attack.

Accusations:
Satan is the accuser of the brethren. In the book of Job it says that the enemy patrols the earth, watching and waiting to find someone to accuse. When someone accuses you of wrongdoing and you are innocent it may cause you to doubt, fear, and cower. Those accusations can cause you mental defeat and lead to things like depression. Are you letting false accusations hinder your purpose?

Stand on God's Truth
DURING A SPIRITUAL BATTLE

- God is still + always in control.
- Satan doesn't have free reign over us.
- Understanding that God even limits the degree that satan can cause us problems.
- The struggle provides an opportunity for deeper faith + a deeper relationship with him.
- This difficulty that you are currently facing will ultimately end up working for your good + will accomplish God's purpose in your life.
- The devil is a liar + he is the one one who causes us doubt discouragement & despair.
- Challenges will still come but even in our hard times we are still free & blessed.

We end up prolonging the process when we fight in our human ways.

Walking in the Spirit

TO WALK IN THE SPIRIT MEANS BEING OBEDIENT WHEN THE SPIRIT PROMPTS YOUR SPIRIT TO DO THE WILL OF GOD.

Hebrews 12:1
THROW OFF ALL HINDERANCES (a thing that provides resistance, delay, or obstruction to your life)

Galatians 6:8
SPEND TIME WITH GOD

Romans 12:1-2
PUT ASIDE THE WORLD AND OFFER YOURSELF TO GOD

Jude 1:20
PRAYING IN THE SPIRIT DAILY

John 4:10
OBEY THE VOICE OF THE HOLY SPIRIT IN BIG AND SMALL THINGS

WAYS TO KEEP PURSUING OUR RELATIONSHIP WITH CHRIST

Our feelings can lead us astray. Cling to Truth!

1. Pray boldly and authentically. Pour out everything that lies in your heart.
2. Listen for His answers. Sometimes we speak and do too much which drowns out the subtle voice of Jesus.
3. Praise God for all He is! Gratitude and praise are powerful weapons against pain.
4. Worship Him even when it's difficult. Maintaining a life of worship keeps our hearts in tune with Him.
5. Read God's Word keeping it sealed in the heart. Learn of the hope within those pages.
6. Replace feelings with Truth. Taking every feeling and thought captive to the Word of God. Re-framing it with the light of His Truth will bring healing and show the traces of God's hand in each step.

Jesus

My King
My Lord
My Savior
My Healer
My Refuge
My Provider
My Strength
My Defender
My Protector
My Peace
My Joy

My Life. My All. My Everything

Prayer of Surrender

I am so grateful for the blessings you have given me. I am thankful for _____. Lord, I surrender my heart to You. I offer up my desires. I place them at the foot of the cross. Fill me with a desire for your will and for Your glory. I surrender my expectations to you today. Help me to place all my hope in you and to be grateful for what I have. Lord, I place my hurts in your hands. Take my burdens and work in me. Heal and redeem my brokenness, Lord. Today I specifically surrender ___ to you. I place it/them at your cross and ask that your will be done. Change my heart to long for your ways.
I am willing, God, to go where You are calling me. I offer up these to You.

                In Jesus Name, Amen.

I have amazing potential
I can make good choices
I am never alone
I can do hard things
I am beautiful inside + out
I am of great worth
He has a plan for me
I know who I am

I am a daughter of God

The closer you walk with God, the less room for anything to come between

Promises of God We Can Count on

HE IS WORKING ALL THINGS FOR OUT GOOD

Romans 8:28

HE WILL COMPLETE HIS WORK

Phillipians 1:6

HE CARRIES US.

Psalm 68:19

HE WILL STRENGTHEN US.

Isaiah 40:31

HIS GRACE IS SUFFICIENT FOR US

2 Corinthians 4:12

HIS GOODNESS IS SATISFYING

Jeremiah 31:14

HE WILL NOT ALLOW YOU TO BE TEMPTED BEYOND YOUR ABILITY.

1 Corinthians 10:13

HE WILL GIVE YOU REST

Matthew 11:28-30

Scriptures

to pray when you don't know what to pray

Give unto the Lord the glory due unto his name: bring an offering, and come before him: worship the Lord in the beauty of holiness.
1 Chronicles 16:29

Therefore confess your sins to each other and pray for each other so that you may be healed. The prayer of a righteous person is powerful and effective.
James 5:16

And without faith it is impossible to please God, because anyone who comes to him must believe that he exists and that he rewards those who earnestly seek him.
Hebrews 11:6

Let us then approach God's throne of grace with confidence, so that we may receive mercy and find grace to help us in our time of need. Hebrews 4:16

This is the confidence we have in approaching God: that if we ask anything according to his will, he hears us. And if we know that he hears us—whatever we ask—we know that we have what we asked of him.
1 John 5:14-15

CHARACTERISTICS OF

Spiritual Growth

DESIRE
Like newborn infants, long for the pure spiritual milk, that by it you may grow up into salvation—if indeed you have tasted that the Lord is good.
1 Peter 2:2-3 ESV

GROWING IN GRACE + KNOWLEDGE:
But grow in the grace and knowledge of our Lord and Savior Jesus Christ. To him be the glory both now and to the day of eternity. Amen.
2 Peter 3:18 ESV

PRACTICES DISCERNMENT, DISTINGUISHING GOOD FROM EVIL
For though by this time you ought to be teachers, you need someone to teach you again the basic principles of the oracles of God. You need milk, not solid food for everyone who lives on milk is unskilled in the word of righteousness, since he is a child.
But solid food is for the mature, for those who have their powers of discernment trained by constant practice to distinguish good from evil.
Hebrews 5:12-14 ESV

CHARACTERISTICS OF
Spiritual Growth

WORSHIPS IN THE HOUSE OF GOD:
The righteous flourish like the palm tree and grow like a cedar in Lebanon. They are planted in the house of the LORD; they flourish in the courts of our God.
Psalm 92:12-13 ESV

BEARS FRUIT (EVEN IN OLD AGE)
They still bear fruit in old age; they are ever full of sap and green.
Psalm 92:14 ESV

ISN'T UNSTABLE BUT SPEAKS TRUTH IN LOVE:
Until we all attain to the unity of the faith and of the knowledge of the Son of God, to mature manhood, to the measure of the stature of the fullness of Christ, so that we may no longer be children, tossed to and fro by the waves and carried about by every wind of doctrine, by human cunning, by craftiness in deceitful schemes.Rather, speaking the truth in love, we are to grow up in every way into him who is the head, into Christ,
Ephesians 4:13-15 ESV

Verses to grow a powerful prayer life

MARK 11:24

1 THESSALONIANS 5:16-19

PHILLIPPIANS 4:6-7

JAMES 5:16

1 JOHN 5: 14-15

"NOTHING ELSE MATTERS. NOTHING ELSE SATISFIES. NOTHING ELSE DESERVES OUR PRAISE. NOTHING BUT GOD – AND SUDDENLY WE HAVE EVERYTHING. EVEN IN THE MIDDLE OF HARDSHIPS."

PRAYERS FOR WHEN YOU ARE
Busy + Stressed

Lord my mind is overwhelmed and I feel that I am all over the place. I feel like I have so much to do . I feel like I work so hard and I am barely getting anything done. I feel like i'm on a hamster wheel and I am getting nowhere. Lord help me when stress fills up inside of me and takes away my peace.

Cast your cares on the LORD and he will sustain you; he will never let the righteous be shaken.
Psalms 55:22

Lord why do I allow my burdens and worry consume me when I can just trust you with it? I pray that you give me freedom in my mind. You say in your word that we don't have be to anxious about anything. I can give my requests and burdens to you.

Cast all your anxiety on him because he cares for you.
1 Peter 5:7

Stressed?

MEDITATE ON THESE SCRIPTURES

JEREMIAH 29:11

PROVERBS 29:11

PROVERBS 3:5-6

EPHESIANS 4:26

EPHESIANS 4:31-32

HEBREWS 12:6

Prayer for Strength

Father,

As you know sometimes I stray away from your word. Stress and anxiety seem to multiply. My body gets tired and stress creeps in. So lord, I ask for strength in my mind.

Lord I pray for the strength that you have promised in your word. I pray for your power to take the next step. I am so thankful because I know that in your strength my weakness is replaced with everything that you are. I receive it it today.

In Jesus Name, Amen

VERSES TO PRAY *When you feel like giving up*

2 CHRONICLES 15:7

PROVERBS 18:10

PHILIPPIANS 4:13

MATTHEW 11:28

EXODUS 14:14

WHENEVER YOU DO NOT UNDERSTAND WHAT IS HAPPENING IN YOUR LIFE, JUST CLOSE YOUR EYES, TAKE A DEEP BREATH AND SAY "GOD, I KNOW IT'S YOUR PLAN. JUST HELP ME THROUGH IT."

When you feel Exhausted

Isaiah 41:13

Matthew 11:30

2 Corinthians 12:9

Psalms 119:114

Galatians 6:9

Apostle Paul tells us that we have the power to renew our minds and put an end to belief system that we no longer want to be identified with.

Romans 12:2

A PRAYER FOR FOCUS

Father God, In the Name of Jesus,

I thank and praise you because you know my heart. So, you already know my desire to grow closer to you.

I pray against every distraction as I choose to focus on you + your word today. Lord, I cannot do anything without you so please teach me how to be still as I seek you today. Please quiet every outside distraction and negative thought. Bring order to every thought that will attempt to pull me away from you.

Thank you so much in advance because I know you are willing to do these things for me. Your word tells me that where I am weak I know that you are strong. I love you. Thank you for loving me in Jesus Name, Amen

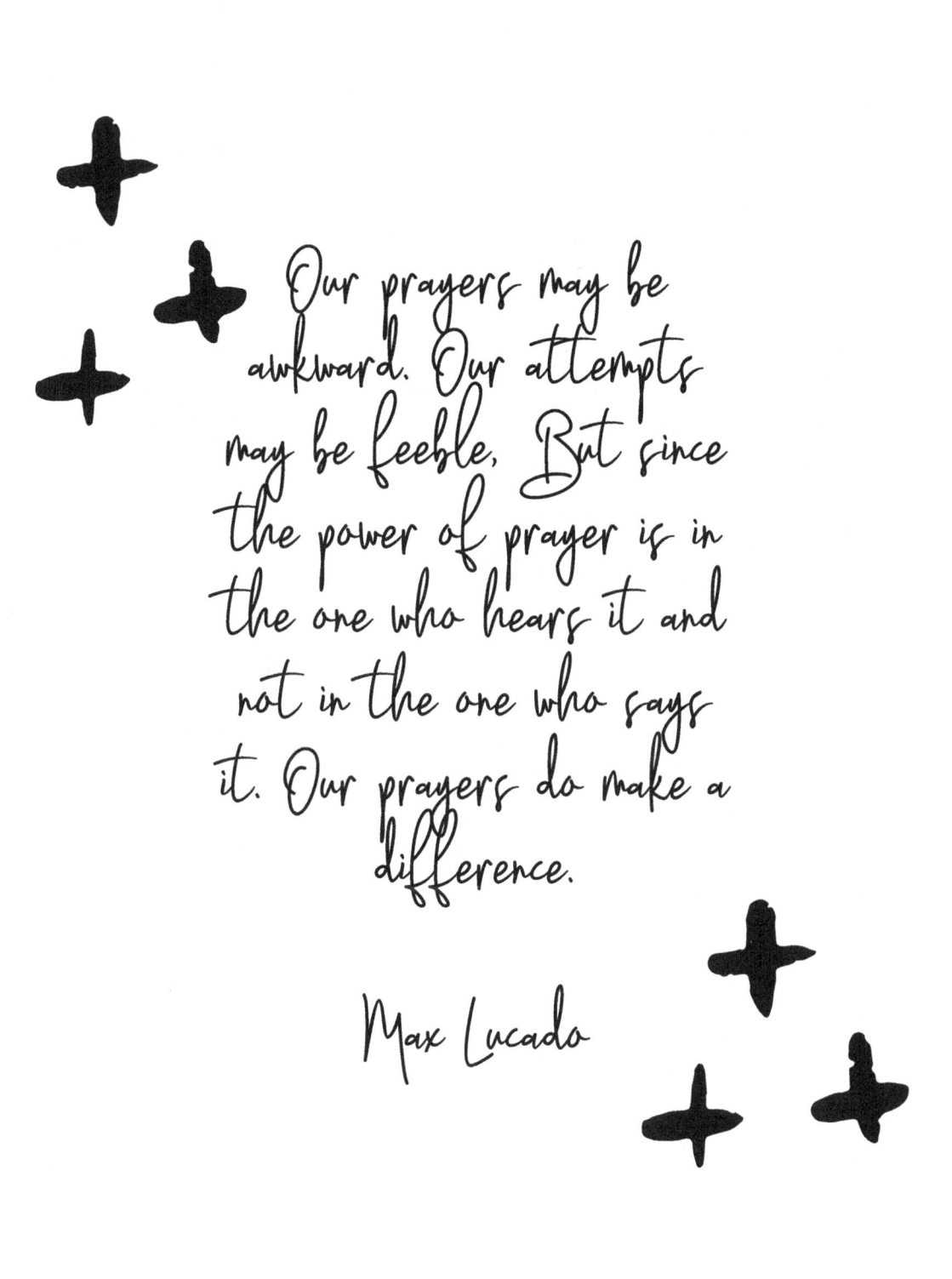

Our prayers may be awkward. Our attempts may be feeble, But since the power of prayer is in the one who hears it and not in the one who says it. Our prayers do make a difference.

Max Lucado

HOW TO LEAD SOMEONE TO CHRIST

First, read Romans 10:9-10 to them (show them the verse either in a bible, on a smartphone, etc.). Next, let them know that they must believe in their heart that Jesus Christ is the Son of God who came to earth to die for our sins in our place and that God raised him from the dead. Then, let them know that they must confess, or say out loud, that "Jesus is my Lord". Finally, pray with them.

SALVATION PRAYER

Dear God,
I know that I am a sinner, and I admit it. I confess with my mouth and believe in my heart that Jesus is Your Son and that He died on the cross for my sins. Jesus, please forgive me for my sins and come into my heart and life and become my personal Lord and Savior. Thank you for hearing my prayer and for saving me. I believe that I am saved.

In Jesus Name, Amen.

Prayer for Unsaved Loved Ones

- Lord please please open _____ eyes, so that they can see you. I pray that you lead them to the truth of your word.
- I ask you to turn + soften _____'s heart. I pray you fill them up with your spirit.
- Lord please draw _____ to you and give him/her a hunger + desire for you.
- Please send a variety of people in _____ path wherever they go so that they can not escape you.
- Please place a hedge of protection around _____ so that any ungodly influences around him/her would lose interest + depart from them.
- Please break any chains, strongholds or barriers that have _____ bound and free them from satan's influence over his/her mind, will + emotions.
- I pray that _____ would be convicted by the Holy Spirit + that he/she would have your thoughts and attitude towards sin.
- Lord, I pray that you let your kindness lead _____ to full repentance and help him/her to turn away from sin.

End all prayers in Jesus Name

PRAYER FOR A FRIEND

Dear God,

I pray for _____. I pray that they may experience new levels of supernatural understanding, strength, endurance, and patience.

I pray that you can give _____ more knowledge of who you are during this season.

In Jesus Name.

PRAYER TO WALK BY FAITH + NOT BY SIGHT

You are the reason why I breathe. You have never failed me. You always keep your word to me.

MY FAITH IN YOU

relies on your character + the truth of your word. not my feelings or emotions. At times my feelings are misleading and my thoughts are negative.

Please grant me the strength through your name to have faith and pray, even when I feel like I want to focus on what I see.

We get our confidence from God

When we lose confidence in trusting God we begin to trust in ourselves and what we can accomplish. Pride and arrogance can take over quick so easily we find ourselves forgetting the goodness and grace of God. Before we know it, something happens or goes wrong that we cannot control and we end up in a place where blame God.

The truth is that nothing apart from God can save us or make us whole. Jesus is the answer and without Him at the center of our lives, we will continue to struggle with having confidence. God's Word is filled with promises of strength and courage if we place our confidence in Jesus Christ.

Confidence Affirmations

PSALM 111:10

I am walking in the wisdom of God

ROMANS 12: 1-2

I choose to live for God and not conform to the ways of the world

EPHESIANS 2:8-9

My worth is not determined by what I have or how well I perform, But by his grace.

TITUS 2:11-12

I am a woman with discipline and self control.

1 CORINTHIANS 2:4-5

My faith isn't based on the wisdom of what I can see but, by the power of God.

PROVERBS 3:3-4

My faith isn't based on the wisdom of what I can see but, by the power of God.

A Prayer for Confidence

Dear God,

I am so thankful because you know my heart. You know that I love you and I am doing my best to follow you. I believe what your word says about me. There are sometimes I get stumble and I lose focus. Sometimes I forget who I am in you and I start looking for the world to tell me who I am.

On the days that I struggling with my confidence, I pray that you will remind me again of who I am in you. Help me remember that my true confidence and self worth can only be found in you.

I speak over myself with the Authority that you have given me through the power of Jesus name:

- I am confident knowing I am loved by you.
- I am confident knowing that in you I am enough.
- I can live confidently knowing that I am called to do great things.

Help me remember all of the promises that you have promised me .

In Jesus Name Amen

Confidence Scriptures

Romans 8:32

Ephesians 2:10

Genesis 1:27

John 16:33

Psalms 46:5

Matthew 20:16

Philippians 1:6

Romans 5:8

Joshua 21:45

"I'm glad in God, far happier than you would ever guess—happy that you're again showing such strong concern for me. Not that you ever quit praying and thinking about me. You just had no chance to show it. Actually, I don't have a sense of needing anything personally. I've learned by now to be quite content whatever my circumstances. I'm just as happy with little as with much, with much as with little. I've found the recipe for being happy whether full or hungry, hands full or hands empty. Whatever I have, wherever I am, I can make it through anything in the One who makes me who I am. I don't mean that your help didn't mean a lot to me—it did. It was a beautiful thing that you came alongside me in my troubles."

- Philippians 4:13 (msg)

Fighting Fear

> "He will never leave you nor forsake you. Do not be afraid; do not be discouraged." Deuteronomy 31:8

When fear tries to overtake you, really envision God saying this, just to you. He's on your side, no matter who leaves after promising they'll be there forever. When friends, family members or co-workers disappoint you. God will never turn on you. My lowest, most painful times been my times of most accelerated time with the Lord.

> "And we know that in all things God works for the good of those who love him, who have been called according to his purpose." Romans 8:28

So much fear is based the enemy illuminating situation to make us think when we've made a mess of situation, it's too late for God's help. God has not only forgiven me after some blatantly unwise, selfish choices, but he's been quick to open doors, answer prayers and pour out more blessings than I could ever deserve.

He's so good. Combat fear by believing he'll turn you situation around for good, simply because he has wonderful purpose for your life, no amount of blunders can hinder.

> Psalm 18:2 "The LORD is my rock, my fortress and my deliverer."

Fear has no place in the heart or mind of a believer. Ask God to increase your trust and faith in his willingness and ability to deliver you completely from fear and anxiety. Ask for a deeper revelation of his love, and watch how powerfully he moves.

If you are

praying about

it. God is

working on it.

Period.

1. START EACH MORNING WITH GRATITUDE YOU ALL OF THE THINGS THAT YOU ALREADY HAVE.

2. GIVE GOD ALL OF YOUR FEARS AND WORRIES.

3. SIMPLY DO SOMETHING NICE FOR SOMEONE ELSE, EXPECTING NOTHING IN RETURN.

4. LET GO OF ANGER AND RESENTMENTS THAT DRAG DOWN YOUR SPIRIT.

5. SHOW YOUR FAMILY MEMBERS AND FRIENDS HOW MUCH YOU APPRECIATE THEM (AGAIN EXPECTING NOTHING IN RETURN.

6. GET RID OF UNNECESSARY MATERIAL POSSESSIONS THAT ARE NOT ESSENTIAL TO YOUR LIFE, ESPECIALLY IF YOU CAN DONATE/BE A BLESSING THEM TO SOMEONE ELSE WHO REALLY NEED IT.

7. END EACH DAY BY THANKING GOD FOR ALL OF THE GOOD THINGS IN YOUR LIFE.

FIND JOY

Pray continually

1 THESSALONIANS 5:17

A Prayer of
forgiveness

Father in the name of Jesus I give _____ to you. I am having a hard time letting go of hurts and offenses. Lord I want to forgive but I cannot do it on my own I need your help. The pain feels too hard for me to let go of.

Lord, I give you that hurt. Lord please heal and restore every part of me that has been and is being affected by this situation.

I release them and all emotions that have been and is still being affected by this situation.

In Jesus Name Amen

personal forgiveness journey

Name of who I need to forgive:

Why am i upset?

They may have done this because.....

I can forgive them Because....

In the future I will....

God forgive me for.....

ASKING GOD FOR PERSONAL FORGIVENESS FOR:

HELP ME TO FORGIVE:

ASKING GOD TO SHOW ME AREAS I MAY BE BLIND TO, THAT I NEED TO PRACTICE FORGIVENESS:

> Do not grieve, for the joy of the Lord is your strength.
> Nehemiah 8:10

WHEN YOU ARE SICK, GOD CALLS YOU HEALTHY. WHEN EVERY ODD IS STACKED AGAINST YOU, GOD SAYS YOU FIGHT FROM VICTORY TO VICTORY. GOD DOESNT CALL YOU WHAT YOU ARE, HE CALLS US WHAT WE WILL BECOME.

Affirmations to Renew Your Mind

PROVERBS 8:14

I have sound knowledge and wisdom. I have might, power and through God who gives me strength.

JOB 12:10

I live and breathe because of Christ who is within me.

2 CORINTHIANS 5:17

Today I am a new creation, I begin again with a clean slate, a fresh mindset and a new start.

JAMES 1:4

I am whole and complete - lacking nothing as I pursue God's purpose for my life.

2 TIMOTHY 1:7

My mind is clear and my focus is sharp. I am full of faith and fearless.

i am his

He is faithful when I am not.

He is constant when I am not.

He is everything when I am nothing.

Yet he says I am his.

a prayer for provision

Father in the name of Jesus,
I sometimes I worry and sometimes I allow anxiety to get the best of me
The enemy tries to whisper to me that my situation in hopeless and you will not come through for me.
But, I trust in your promises...
I cling with my life to your character
You are the Lord who provides
I know your ways are higher than mine and your thoughts higher than my thoughts!
You may not come the way that I expect it but I do know that you will come through.
Help me to seek your will for my life
Not just what I want
Not even what I think that I need.
Help me to just seek you.
Not your hand but your will for my life.
I release all of my worries and plans, my fears for the future and my doubts + my fears to you!
Thank you in advance
In Jesus Name Amen!

She who kneels before God can stand before anything

Verses to Pray over your finances

And my God will supply all of my needs according to his riches in Glory.
Philippians 4:19

And do not seek what you to eat and what you are to drink, nor be worried... your father knows that you need them. Instead, seek His kingdom, and these things will be added unto you.
Luke 12: 29-31

In all toil there is profit but mere talk only leads to poverty
Proverbs 14:23

In all things that I have shown you by working hard in this way we must help the weak and remember the words of the Lord Jesus, how he himself said, 'It is more blessed to give than receive.
Acts 20:35

I know how to be brought low, and I know how to be abound. In any circumstance, I have learned the secret of facing plenty and hunger in the abundance and need. I can do all things through Christ that strengthens me.
Philippians 4:12-13

faith tells me that no matter what lies ahead god is already there!

The concept of spiritual rest is one of those things that can be really hard for people to grasp.

It's not just about sleeping. a lot of restlessness is not just a physical issue but an emotional/spiritual issue.

We are constantly bombarded by things that want to steal our peace and cause us stress.

UNDERSTANDING
Spiritual Rest

Rest Scriptures

My presence will go with you, and I will give you rest.
Exodus 33:14

My soul finds rest in God alone; my salvation comes from him. He alone is my rock and my salvation; he is my fortress, I will never be shaken.
Psalm 62:1-2

Do you not know? Have you not heard? The Lord is the everlasting God, the Creator of the ends of the earth. He will not grow tired or weary, and his understanding no one can fathom. He gives strength to the weary and increases the power of the weak. Even youths grow tired and weary, and young men stumble and fall; but those who hope in the Lord will renew their strength. They will soar on wings like eagles; they will run and not grow weary, they will walk and not be faint.
Isaiah 40:28-31

Whoever dwells in the shelter of the Most High, will rest in the shadow of the Almighty. I will say of the Lord, "He is my refuge and my fortress, my God, in whom I trust.
Psalm 91:1-2

The fear of the Lord leads to life; then one rests content, untouched by trouble.
Proverbs 19:23

Return to your rest, my soul, for the Lord has been good to you. – Psalm 116:7
This is what the Lord says: Stand at the crossroads and look; ask for the ancient paths, ask where the good way is, and walk in it, and you will find rest for your souls. But you said, 'We will not walk in it.'
Jeremiah 6:16

The fear of the LORD leads to life, So that one may sleep satisfied, untouched by evil. – Proverbs 19:23

The Lord is my shepherd, I lack nothing. He makes me lie down in green pastures, he leads me beside quiet waters.
Psalm 23:1-2

FIGHT BACK AGAINST SHAME + COMPARSION

**I am so thankful to be a broken vessel so that your power along with everything I need can shine though.
Write out 2 Corinthians 4:7**

I refuse to life a life of comparison because it only leads to comparison 2 corinthians 10:12; but instead I attempt to imitate you 1 Corinthians 11:1

**You are the only one who defines me! You call me wonderful + marvelous
Psalms 139:13-14**

**My weakness are made strong through you. Write out
2 Corinthians 12:9**

**I have no need to fear because you have great plans for me.
2 timothy 1:7**

You are the only one who defines me! You call me wonderful + marvelous
Psalms 139:13-14

My weakness are made strong through you. Write out
2 Corinthians 12:9

I have no need to fear because you have great plans for me.
2 timothy 1:7

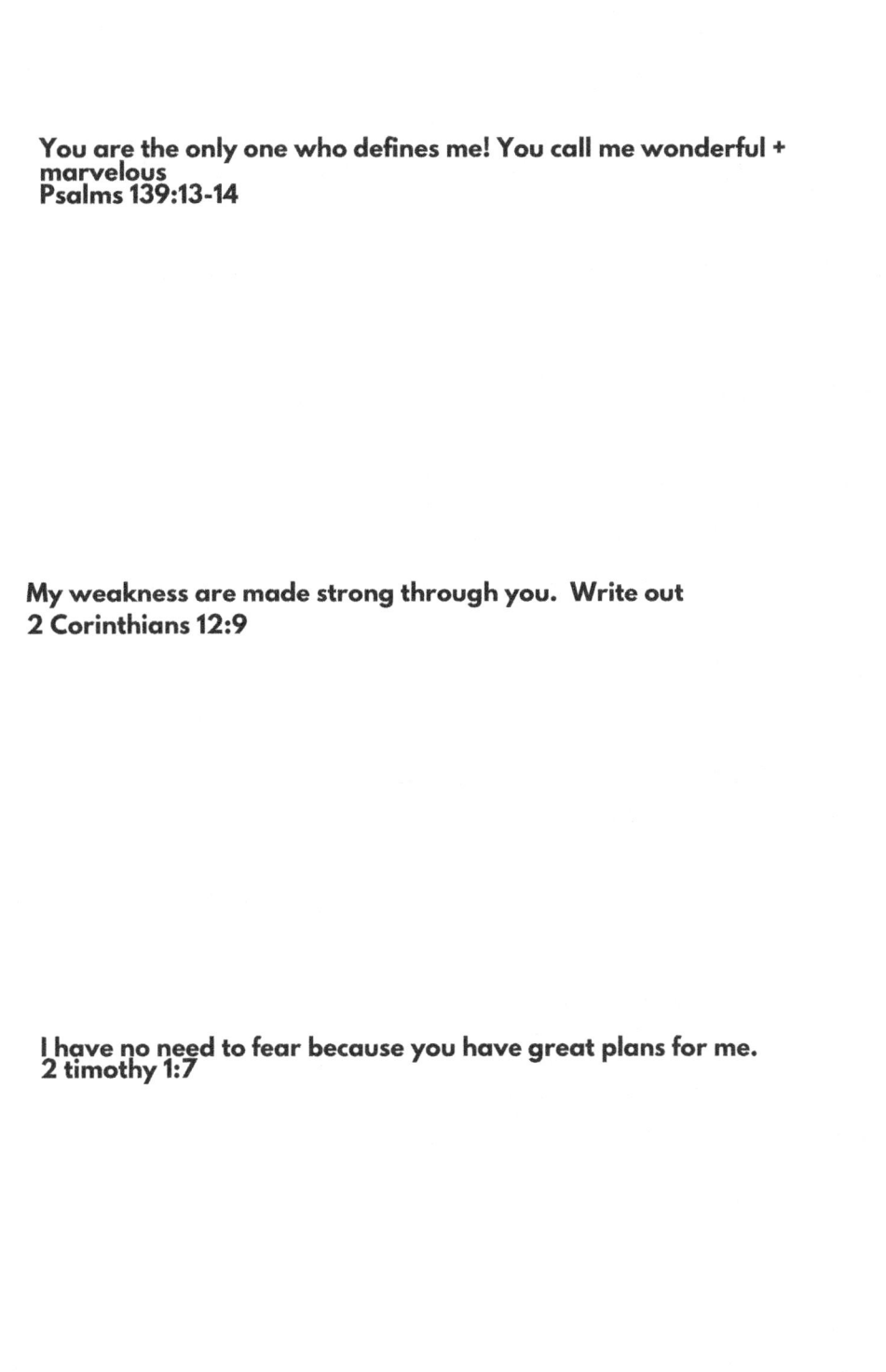

Love Yourself God's Way

- Remember you are valued and precious to God.
- Know, accept, and be yourself.
- Forgive yourself like God forgives you.
- Treat yourself with care and compassion.
- Care for your physical needs . . . diet, move and rest.
- Refuse to waste time on stinkin' thinkin'.
- Ask for help when you need it.
- Sing, dance, and laugh more.
- Refuse to speak unkind words to yourself.
- Say 'no' when you need to.
- Do something you were created to do every day.
- Pursue your hopes and dreams.
- Be honest with yourself and others.
- Pray – ask God to help you know your strengths.
- Pray – ask God to show you your weaknesses.
- Pray – ask God for His guidance and help.
- Stop and give thanks for your life every day.
- Spend time with people you love.
- Accept what you can't change.
- Forgive others.
- Be bold and try something new.
- Believe God has a plan and purpose for you.
- Live engaged in every moment.
- Be patient with yourself.
- Be still – know and love God.

WHEN YOU FEEL *Rejected*

The LORD will not reject his people; he will not abandon his special possession. Psalms 94:14

Though my father and mother forsake me, the LORD will receive me. Psalms 27:10

Cast all your anxiety on him because he cares for you. 1 Peter 5:7

Do not be afraid of them, for I am with you and will rescue you," declares the Lord. Jeremiah 1:8

So don't be afraid; you are worth more than many sparrows. Matthew 10:31

If the world hates you, keep in mind that it hated me first. John 15:18

He rescues me unharmed from the battle waged against me, even though many oppose me. Psalms 55:18

"I, yes I, am the one who comforts you. So why are you afraid of mere humans, who wither like the grass and disappear?
Isaiah 51:12

When hard pressed, I cried to the LORD; he brought me into a spacious place.
Psalm 118:5

Prayer Against Self - defeat

Father God in the Name of Jesus,
I pray against every lie that the enemy attempts to whisper to me that is opposite of your truth.

When the enemy attempts to tell me that I'm in a hopeless situation, tries to cause confusion and make situations bigger than they really are by telling me that I will never make it and attempt to surround me with negative thoughts and fear.

I ask you to help me see you and your will for my life. Help me to find a safe place in your word. Give me spiritual eyes to see your truth. I pray that you will replace my fear with unwavering faith in your promises.
Remind me that I surrounded by your love. The truth is nothing can stop your love. Help me see myself the way that you see me. Thank you that by your name I have authority to cast out the lies and darkness that attempt to tell me that I am not enough.

I pray that you drown out all of the noise and chaos and that your plans will occupy my mind validate my worth.

In Jesus Name Amen.

OVERCOMING BITTERNESS 1

Hebrews 12:14-15
Strive for peace with everyone, and for the holiness without which no one will see the Lord. See to it that no one fails to obtain the grace of God; that no "root of bitterness" springs up and causes trouble, and by it many become defiled;

Bitterness is toxic. It's a cancer. It will spread and grow. Bitterness can contaminate your entire generational line. Bitter people tend to pass bitterness on to their children. We have to get it out. It must be uprooted. The only way to get rid of bitterness is through forgiveness.

Ephesians 4:31
Let all bitterness and wrath and anger and clamor and slander be put away from you, along with all malice.

Living free of bitterness requires repentance. Remember that "repent" means to change the way you think. When it comes to bitterness, you are going to have to change the way you think. This verse says that we need to put away bitterness, wrath, anger, clamor and malice. Sounds like a lot but we wouldn't be instructed to rid ourselves of these things if God hadn't given us the power and ability to do so.

Ephesians 4:32
Be kind to one another, tenderhearted, forgiving one another, as God in Christ forgave you.

Verse 31 told us what to put away but verse 32 tell us what to put on! Kindness, tenderheartedness and forgiveness. Forgiveness can be a tough thing to give. Bitterness is almost like this weird man made shield. We hide behind it in order to avoid dealing with the pain that other have caused us. The truth is that it isn't a very good shield! Your shield is poisoning you.

OVERCOMING BITTERNESS 2

Matthew 18:21-22
Then Peter came up and said to him, "Lord, how often will my brother sin against me, and I forgive him? As many as seven times?" Jesus said to him, "I do not say to you seven times, but seventy-seven times.

I think that it is important to acknowledge that God doesn't tell us to forgive others because He's just some mean and insensitive Father that is trying to write off and make less of our hurts. God cares about your pain. He tells you to forgive because resentment and bitterness hurt you more than they hurt others. They are man made prisons and He wants you to be free.

Luke 7:47
Therefore I tell you, her sins, which are many, are forgiven—for she loved much. But he who is forgiven little, loves little."

My greatest advice for overcoming just about anything is to intentionally meditate and think on the fact that you have been completely forgiven. God has forgiven the unforgivable in you and He tells you that you are able to forgive others. Through partnering with Him you can live free from bitterness and resentment.

John 16:33
I have said these things to you, that in me you may have peace. In the world you will have tribulation. But take heart; I have overcome the world."

Life is hard and people are complicated and difficult. But God is good and He is faithful and He has paid an ultimate price to give you hope, peace and a future. There is life in Him. Bitterness has it's roots in the opposite of life.

WHAT TO DO WITH FEELINGS OF
injustice and bitterness

1. Trust God to use the situation for good
(Romans 8:28).

2. Put your hope in God alone, not circumstances or earthly justice
(Psalm 62).

3. Focus on the good things in your life
(Philippians 4:8).

4. When unproductive thoughts overtake you, pray for your offender. And, if God prompts you to bless your offender in some tangible way, obey Him
(Romans 12:14, 17-21).

5. Refuse false blame from Satan
(1 Peter 5:8,9).

6. But listen carefully to God's conviction and genuinely repent of any sinful attitudes or actions you have, no matter how small in comparison to your offender
(1 John 1:9).

7. Release all bitterness by the power of God's Spirit because you can't do it on your own
Ephesians 3:20-21; Philippians 4:13).

8. Remind yourself that you are doing these things because you love Christ and owe Him your life
(1 Corinthians 6:20).

For the Lord is the Spirit, and wherever the Spirit of the Lord is, there is freedom.

2 Corinthians 3:17

peace

The Lord will give strength to His people;
The Lord will bless His people with peace.
Psalm 29:11 NKJV

Prayer Declaration:
Lord, thank you for your promise to give me strength. I trust that You will provide it right when I need it. No matter what I'm feeling or what situation I am in, I can be confident that You will bless me with peace. I refuse to let anything steal that peace, knowing that whatever comes my way, You have it under control.
In Jesus' name, Amen.

You will keep in perfect peace those whose minds are steadfast, because they trust in you.
Isaiah 26:3 NIV

Prayer Declaration:
Thank you, Lord that You will keep me in perfect peace as my mind stays focused on you. Help me to trust in You. Teach me Your promises, that I may cling to them in times of need. Let my mind meditate on the truth of Your Word, rather than on feelings based on what I see in the natural. In Jesus' name, Amen.

I've told you all this so that trusting me, you will be unshakable and assured, deeply at peace. In this godless world you will continue to experience difficulties. But take heart! I've conquered the world.
John 16:33 MSG

Prayer Declaration:
Father, thank you that you are faithful. You are true to Your Word and trustworthy. When I begin to doubt, remind me of all You've done for me. I can be confident in all things, because You have overcome every obstacle, including death. Thank You for Your perfect sacrifice, that gives me perfect peace. In Jesus' name, Amen.

PRAYER
FOR A PEACEFUL MIND

This day + everyday I condemn the thoughts that the enemy sends to penetrate my mind. I boldly confess that the enemy is defeated and does not have any power or authority over me.

I pray that as your scripture promises me, No weapon Formed against me will prosper. Lord I thank you because every word of your promise is true. I confess that I believe your words + your plans toward me. In Jesus Name Amen.

PRAYER
for a peaceful home

Lord, I thank you for the home that you blessed me with. I pray that as people come in they will feel your peace that surpasses all understanding.

I pray that if people come in feeling overwhelmed, they will leave with your peace in their hearts and in their minds.

Help us to create an atmostphere that your Holy Spirit will abide and that others would love to come.

In Jesus name, Amen

It's okay to

pray

FOR EXACTLY WHAT YOUR HEART DESIRES

Prayer for PATIENCE

Lord,

Thank you for the many blessings in my life right now. Open my eyes to each gift you have given me. I know my heart can be so quick to become impatient. It can be fear, frustration, exhaustion or so many other things that seem to zap my patience and my energy. Lord, I know that You provide the strength I need to be patient. Holy Spirit, I ask that You work in me today. Open my heart to Your love and sufficiency in every area of my life. Fill me with the strength and peace I need to be patient today. Develop the fruit of patience in my heart.

In Jesus Name, Amen.

TAMING YOUR TONGUE

The Bible says we all stumble when it comes to our words. They can build others up or tear them down.

"Whoever of you loves life and desires to see many good days, keep your tongue from evil and your lips from telling lies."
Psalm 34:12-13

"The mouth of the righteous is a fountain of life…"
Proverbs 10:11

"Sin is not ended by multiplying words, but the prudent hold their tongues." Proverbs 10:19

"The lips of the righteous nourish many…" Proverbs 10:21

"From the mouth of the righteous comes the fruit of wisdom, but a perverse tongue will be silenced."Proverbs 10:31

"Whoever derides their neighbor has no sense, but the one who has understanding holds their tongue." Proverbs 11:12

"The words of the reckless pierce like swords, but the tongue of the wise brings healing." Proverbs 12:18

"A gentle answer turns away wrath, but a harsh word stirs up anger." Proverbs 15:1

"The soothing tongue is a tree of life, but a perverse tongue crushes the spirit." Proverbs 15:4

"The hearts of the wise make their mouths prudent, and their lips promote instruction. Gracious words are a honeycomb, sweet to the soul and healing to the bones." Proverbs 16:23-24

PRAYERS TO FIGHT

A FOUL MOUTH

Father God I ask you in the name of Jesus to help me so that no corrupt word will come out of my mouth.
Ephesians 4:29

Father God I ask you in the name of Jesus to help me so that my speech will always be graceful and that I may know how I ought to answer everyone
Colossians 4:6

Father God I ask you in the name of Jesus to help me so that words of my mouth and the meditations of my heart be acceptable you.
Psalms 19:14

"Praise be to the Lord, the God of Israel, because he has come to his people and redeemed them.

Luke 1:68

MAKING DECISIONS GOD'S WAY

CONSIDER PRAYING OVER EACH QUESTION AND THEN AND LISTEN FOR GOD'S ANSWERS. THE PROCESS CAN TAKE TIME, SO TRY NOT TO RUSH IT.

- What can I do to receive God's words in this situation? Am I reading my Bible regularly?
Proverbs 2:1

- What is the truth based on the Bible? How can I treasure it?
Proverbs 2:1

- What can I do to listen well to God?
Proverbs 2:2

- Am I praying for discernment? Could I ask others to pray for me as I seek an answer?
Proverbs 2:3

- What can I do to keep seeking wisdom in this situation?
Proverbs 2:4

Faith doesn't exempt us from lifes difficulties, the storms of life come to every person. God will not allow a storm unless he has a divine purpose for it.

Wisdom

We should all be praying and asking God for on a daily basis. King Solomon is considered the wisest man that ever lived, because he asked God for wisdom instead of anything else in his Kingdom. As a result, God granted him riches and fame and all the other blessings that he didn't even ask for from the Father.

The prophet Daniel explains that all wisdom comes from God as he writes, "Blessed be the name of God forever and ever, to whom belong wisdom and might" (Daniel 2:20). We too need wisdom in our lives to make the best decisions,

"The fear of the Lord is the beginning of wisdom; all those who practice it have a good understanding. His praise endures forever!" Psalm 111:10

"Blessed is the one who finds wisdom, and the one who gets understanding," Proverbs 3:13

"And it is my prayer that your love may abound more and more, with knowledge and all discernment..." Philippians 1:9

Let the word of Christ dwell in you richly, teaching and admonishing one another in all wisdom, singing psalms and hymns and spiritual songs, with thankfulness in your hearts to God." Colossians 3:16

"But solid food is for the mature, for those who have their powers of discernment trained by constant practice to distinguish good from evil." Hebrews 5:14

"If any of you lacks wisdom, let him ask God, who gives generously to all without reproach, and it will be given him." James 1:5

"But the wisdom from above is first pure, then peaceable, gentle, open to reason, full of mercy and good fruits, impartial and sincere."
James 3:17

Dream big. Think of the Bible heroes you have admired all your life: Abraham, Moses, David, Paul. They were men of courage and faith who accomplished great things—with God's help.

The light of God
surrounds me.
The love of God
enfolds me.
The power of God
Protects me
The presence of God
watches over me
Wherever I am, God is

He Heals
The wounds of a shattered heart
Psalms 147:3

PRAY OVER YOURSELF

Your Mind - Psalms 42:5

Your Faith - Ephesians 3:12

Your Friends - Proverbs 12:26

Your Husband - Ephesians 5:22

Your Influences - 1 John 2:15

PRAYER OF PRAISE AND GUIDANCE

Father God in the Name of Jesus,

I pray that you tear down all strongholds in my life. I need you because without you I am nothing. God without me, you are still God, but me without you, I am nothing.

Help me not to just pray words because the sound nice but help me to execute the actions to follow. I ask you for forgiveness not only in my life but in the lives of my family and friends as well.

I pray for deliverance and guidance everyday. God please give me the faith that I need to believe that you can do it.

In Jesus Name Amen.

YOUR BEAUTY SHOULD BE THAT OF YOUR INNER SELF, WITH THE UNFADING BEAUTY OF A GENTLE AND QUIET SPIRIT WHICH IS OF GREAT WORTH IN GODS SIGHT!

1 Peter 3:4

WAR ROOM PRAYERS

I am Loved.
John 3:16

I am Forgiven.
Matthew 26:27-28

I am Chosen.
1 Peter 2:9

Gods lights up my steps.
Psalms 119:105

We have protective armor.
Ephesians 6:10-18

Holy Spirit intercedes for me.
Romans 8:26-27

Greater God within me than he who is in the World
1 John 4:4

The Lord is my help
Psalms 121

Praise silences the enemy.
Psalms 8:1-3

God is working it all out for my Good
Romans 8:28

When it's hard to Pray
Prayer Prompts

Father, I thank you for the gift of salvation. I know that you love me and are working for my good. Thank you for what You are doing in my life right now that I cannot see. Amen.

Dear God, I am hurting right now, but I offer my hurting heart to You. I surrender control to You and I ask that You please fill me with the strength to get through today. Amen.

Heavenly Father, I don't know what today holds but I know that You do. You love me deeply and care for me in this moment. Give me strength to walk through today in Your grace. Amen.

Lord, I know your plan is good. Help me to believe that in my heart. Change my heart to be like Yours. I want to follow You in everything I do today. Show me Your way. Amen.

Gracious God, I have fallen short. I am afraid of what's to come. Take my fear and heal my heart. Remind me of Your promises and Your grace. Step into my heart and provide me with the strength to move forward in faith. Amen.

Heavenly Father, I ask that You would strengthen me today. Open my eyes to Your will and give me the grace and energy that I need to obey you. Remind me of your grace and love. Amen.

Psalms 103

Praise the Lord, my soul; all my inmost being, praise his holy name. Praise the Lord, my soul, and forget not all his benefits— who forgives all your sins and heals all your diseases, who redeems your life from the pit and crowns you with love and compassion, who satisfies your desires with good things so that your youth is renewed like the eagle's. The Lord works righteousness and justice for all the oppressed. Psalm 103 He made known his ways to Moses, his deeds to the people of Israel: The Lord is compassionate and gracious, slow to anger, abounding in love. He will not always accuse, nor will he harbor his anger forever; he does not treat us as our sins deserve or repay us according to our iniquities. For as high as the heavens are above the earth, so great is his love for those who fear him; as far as the east is from the west, so far has he removed our transgressions from us. As a father has compassion on his children, so the Lord has compassion on those who fear him; for he knows how we are formed, he remembers that we are dust. The life of mortals is like grass, they flourish like a flower of the field; the wind blows over it and it is gone, and its place remembers it no more. But from everlasting to everlasting the Lord's love is with those who fear him, and his righteousness with their children's children—with those who keep his covenant and remember to obey his precepts. The Lord has established his throne in heaven, and his kingdom rules over all. Praise the Lord, you his angels, you mighty ones who do his bidding, who obey his word. Praise the Lord, all his heavenly hosts, you his servants who do his will. Praise the Lord, all his works everywhere in his dominion. Praise the Lord, my soul.

1. **Illuminates the Word**

For the believer, the Holy Spirit turns what many consider a scholarly, ancient text into a living, breathing letter from God (Hebrews 4:12). He provides a greater depth of understanding we previously lacked before faith, giving purpose to every passage.

As Jesus said: "When the Spirit of truth comes, He will guide you into all the truth. For He will not speak on His own, but He will speak whatever He hears. He will also declare to you what is to come." John 16:13

2. Applies the Word in our Heart

Once we see intent behind a portion of Scripture, the Holy Spirit then convicts our heart. He may show us outright sin that lies there—whether it be our failure to do what God has asked (sins of omission, i.e. failing to witness to others), or do what He forbids (sins of commission, i.e. lying).

When we resist these convictions and calls, we are walking in the flesh. Being faithful to be in the Word, to spend "quiet time" with God, softens our heart to His will and gives us greater opportunity to walk with the Spirit.

"I say then, walk by the Spirit and you will not carry out the desire of the flesh. 17 For the flesh desires what is against the Spirit, and the Spirit desires what is against the flesh; these are opposed to each other, so that you don't do what you want. 18But if you are led by the Spirit, you are not under the law." Galatians 5:16-18

3. Magnifies the Grace of Christ

Lastly, as we behold God's truth, acknowledging our unworthiness and sin, the Holy Spirit lovingly points us to Jesus. We see Christ's mercy at the cross and stunning resurrection, once again showing us their infinite worth and promising us hope.

Even in the darkest of passages, the Holy Spirit finds a way to exalt Christ, and reminds us how He redefines our entire life.

"[The Holy Spirit] will glorify Me, because He will take from what is Mine and declare it to you." John 16:1

SOMETIMES ITS NOT ABOUT THE ANSWER TO THE PRAYER; BUT WHAT YOU LEARN IN THE PROCESS

PRAYER FOR WHEN YOU STRUGGLE WITH

WEIGHT GAIN

Father God in the Name of Jesus,
I humbly come to your for help. You know that I desire to be healthy. I want to be free from my struggle with eating and weight gain.

You know my heart and everything about me, so help me to see myself the way that you see me as your child. Let me find strength and acceptance in your love.

Help me as I pray right now to start with small steps forward. Help me to find the courage and strength in you and in your love for me.
In you all things are possible. Left me find my comfort and satisfaction in you when I want to turn to food.

In Jesus Name Amen

I loved you at your darkest

ROMANS 5:8

PRAYER AGAINST NEGATIVITY

Heavenly Father,

I pray in the name of Jesus that you will give me your peace so that my mind can find rest in you. Father I pray in the name of Jesus that you will break every chain of negative thoughts that attempt to consume my thinking. I pray that when negative things people have spoken over me try to creep back in you will silence the lies of the enemy.

I pray that you will surround me with positivity and peace. I thank you because your word says that the power of life and death is in our tongue. So I speak in your authority that every stronghold that has produced negativity over my life is broken in the name of Jesus. I submit my thought patterns to you. I pray that you give me the mind and thoughts of Christ in Jesus Name Amen.

When you feel lonely

Dear Father,

Thank you for listening to my prayers. Thank you for you patience with me. Thank you for being with me when I feel so alone. Thank you for being with me during the times it feels like no one around me understands.

Thank you for being with me when I feel like I am in a room full of people, and I still feel alone.

Your promises tell me that I am never alone and its true. Though, I just feel loneliness in my human form, I trust that you will help me by your supernatural power - sense your presence in my life in a way more than I can imagine or even fathom on my own.

In Jesus Name Amen

Don't be the woman who goes to people when you are under attack. Put your phone away and pick up your bible. God's words are the only thing that can truly satisfy us + give us what we need.

Prayer for a
HUMBLE HEART

I pray in the name of Jesus that you will show me faults that I cannot see. God I pray that you will help me with the ones that I can see. Help me in the places that I have been wounded. Help me with the things that make me afraid. I pray that you will help me in the areas that I feel defensive. Help me to remember that I am fearfully and wonderfully made when I want to shrink or hide.

I pray that your Spirit will consume me and work in my inner most parts. Help me to understand what it truly means to operate in humility by your standards. Please cleanse me and heal me. Help me to not be afraid. You were wounded for me and today I give you mine wounds. Please set me free in humility. I pray that I may experience the next level of freedom in you.

In Jesus Name Amen

"Faith is deliberate confidence in the character of God whose ways you may not understand at the time

Oswald Chambers

The LORD will fight for you; you need only to be still."
Exodus 14:14

MARRIAGE PRAYER
For Joy

Dear Heavenly Father,

I pray that you bless our marriage with an overwhelming amount of Joy. We started off strong, and its our deepest desire that we continue to stay that way.

Holy Spirit we invite you into our marriage. We want you to be the center. We want to honor you and enjoy this journey that you have us on together. I pray that you continue to remind us to choose joy over sorrow. As long as we are living I pray that you help us to dwell in your peace and joy.

In Jesus Name, Amen.

CHRIST CENTERED *Marriage*

♥ **JESUS AT THE CENTER**
2 Corinthians 6:14

♥ **HUMBLE AND GENTLE**
Matthew 11:29

♥ **FORGIVENESS**
Ephesians 2:8

♥ **HEALTHY COMMINICATION**
James 5:16

♥ **SACRIFICE**
Ephesians 5:25

♥ **INTIMACY**
Genesis 2:24

♥ **HOPE IN THE LORD**
Romans 10:11

PRAY + GET SOME REST. GOD IS HANDLING WITH WHAT YOU ARE WRESTLING WITH.

Sickness Prayer

Father God,

I lift up all everyone who is facing an illness today, I ask you that you would bring healing, comfort + peace to their body.

Lord I ask that you calm their fears and let them experience the healing power of your love.

In Jesus Name, Amen.

There is so much power in

PERSISTENT PRAYER

Micah 7:7

Defining Your Purpose

YOUR GIFTS AND TALENTS ARE THE BLUEPRINT TO YOUR CALLING

ROMANS 12:3-8

1 CORINTHIANS 12:4-11

1 PETER 4:10-11

JEREMIAH 1:4-5

EPHESIANS 4:8-14

1 PETER 4:10-11

List ways you can be more faithful and obedient to God

PRAY JEREMIAH 29:11 OVER YOUR LIFE

Write Out

PSALMS 23 AND MEDITATE ON IT

PRAY THAT YOU WILL CONTINUALLY WALK CLOSER TO THE LORD

Come close to God, and God will come close to you. Wash your hands, you sinners; purify your hearts, for your loyalty is divided between God and the world. James 4:8

CREATE A PRAYER ASKING GOD TO BRING JOY INTO YOUR LIFE.

PRAY FOR COURAGE TO DO SOMETHING DIFFERENT, YOU CAN DO IT AFRAID, WITH CHRIST

So be strong and courageous! Do not be afraid and do not panic before them (Deuteronomy 31:6).

For God has not given us a spirit of fear and timidity, but of power, love, and self-discipline (2 Timothy 1:7).

forgiveness PRAYER

**Today I make the choice to give it to you.
(Tell him directly what they did + how it makes you feel)**

PRAY FOR A HEART THAT FORGIVES
ASK GOD TO SHOW YOU THE AREAS YOU HAVE DEVELOPED BITTERNESS. ASK FOR A HEART THAT FORGIVES.

Write a prayer asking God for wisdom in your finances.

WRITE OUT A PRAYER OF PRAISE FOR ALL GOD HAS DONE IN YOUR LIFE. MAKE A LIST OF THE TIMES HE HAS COME THROUGH FOR YOU. THANK HIM FOR IT AND WHAT HE WILL DO FOR YOU IN THE FUTURE.

x x x x x x x x x x x x x x x x x x x x

PRAY FOR GOD TO SHED LIGHT ON THE SIN IN YOUR LIFE
SIN HIDDEN IN YOUR HEART, BURIED IN YOUR THOUGHTS

For all have sinned, and come short of the glory of God; Being justified freely by his grace through the redemption that is in Christ Jesus: Whom God hath set forth to be a propitiation through faith in his blood, to declare his righteousness for the remission of sins that are past, through the forbearance of God;
Romans 3:23-25

Praying for peace....
List out all of the areas you need peace + ask God to take control.

Prayer to Tame Your Tongue

**Let your conversation be gracious and attractive so that you will have the right response for everyone (Colossians 4:6).
It is not what goes into your mouth that defiles you; you are defiled by the words that come out of your mouth (Matthew 15:11).**

What dreams have you given up on? Write a prayer based on your dreams & submit your request to God to do what he called you to do.

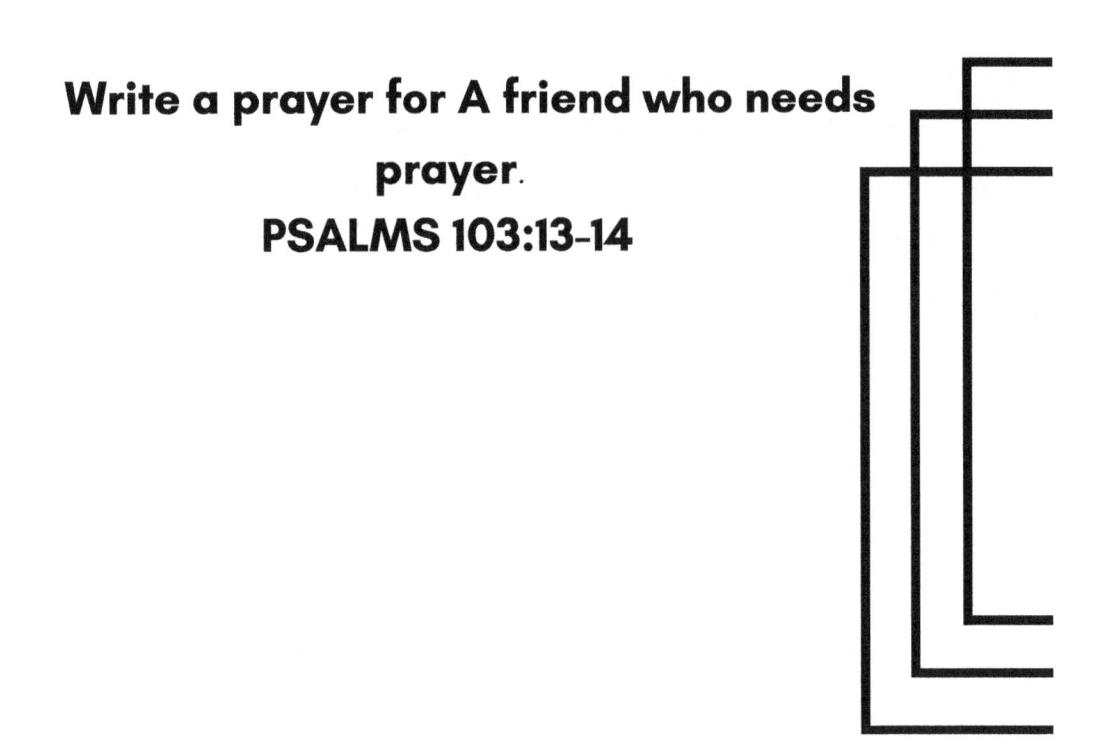

Write a prayer for A friend who needs prayer.
PSALMS 103:13-14

PRAY FOR CONTENTMENT

PSALM 37:16

What areas of your life would you like to grow in right now?
Create a prayer asking God to help you.

Where are you lacking confidence?

Create a prayer asking God to give you boldness & courage.

Fighting FEAR

WHAT IS SOMETHING YOU'VE BEEN AFRAID TO DO? PRAY FOR THE COURAGE TO DO IT.

PHILIPPIANS 4:6-7

ASK GOD TO RENEW YOUR MIND

IDENTIFY FEELINGS OF SHAME +
PRAY TO FIGHT BACK AGAINST SHAMEFUL
FEELINGS. SHAME ISNT FROM GOD.
Psalms 34:5

Where have you been rejected? Write about where you feel you have been rejected + Replace those areas with Gods truth.

John 8:44

List & Pray for things you're embarrassed about

Psalm 112:7

Read, Meditate + Journal
1 Peter 1:8-9

Pray for something you need to release and currently trust God with.

Pray for Your town/city

2 Chronicles 7:14

Meditate + Write a Prayer
ABOUT ROMANS 14:17

Journal About
PSALMS 30:5

pray for

**A PERSON YOU HAVE CHALLENGES
GETTING ALONG WITH**
Matthew 5:44

PRAY
for your health & the health of everyone
your family.

Pray for Miracles
DEUTERONOMY 10:21

**Pray for the presence of
The Beatitudes in your life.**
Matthew 5

Write a prayer for a strong, wise mind, rooted and grounded in Christ....
___

HOW CAN I USE HURT AND PAIN THAT I HAVE GONE THROUGH TO BRING GLORY TO GOD?

LORD I RELEASE _____ TO YOU

A PRAYER OF RELEASE AND SURRENDER

list + pray over all of your goals

For God has not given us a spirit of fear, but of power + of love and of a sound mind.
2 Timothy 1:7

FOR SPECIFICALLY FOR AN AREA OF YOUR LIFE THAT YOU HAVE FEAR.

PRAY TO DEVELOP A HEART AND PRACTICE FOR PRAISE AND WORSHIP

"Holy, holy, holy is the Lord God Almighty, who was, and is, and is to come." Whenever the living creatures give glory, honor, and thanks to him who sits on the throne and who lives forever and ever, the twenty-four elders fall down before him who sits on the throne and worship him who lives forever and ever (Revelations 4: 8-10).

Write a prayer of thanks for the small everyday blessings that we have but often take for granted.

PRAY FOR AN UNDIVIDED HEART THAT IS DEVOTED TO THE LORD.

WRITE A THANK YOU NOTE TO GOD FOR SOMETHING YOU FEEL ESPECIALLY BLESSED THAT HE HAS DONE FOR YOU

USE WORDS OR PHRASES AS IF YOU ARE TALKING TO YOUR BEST FRIEND.

PRAY FOR PEACE IN ALL OF YOUR RELATIONSHIPS

And the peace of God, which surpasses all understanding, will guard your hearts and your minds in Christ Jesus.

Philippians 4:7

WHAT DO YOU FEEL PASSIONATELY ABOUT? WHERE DO YOU SENSE GOD CALLING YOU TO TAKE ACTION?

PRAY FOR PROTECTION AGAINST THE ENEMY....

Strengthen us in the power of Your might, O God. Dress us in Your armor so that we can stand firm against the schemes of the devil. We know that our struggle is not against flesh and blood, but against the rulers, against the powers, against the world forces of this darkness, against the spiritual forces of wickedness in the heavenly places.
Ephesians 6:10-12

PRAY FOR A DEEPER UNDERSTANDING OF GODS WORD

Call to me and I will answer you and tell you great and unsearchable things you do not know.
Jeremiah 33.3

PRAY

FOR A CONTINUAL HUNGER OF GODS WORD + COMMUNICATING WITH OUR FATHER THROUGH PRAYER

Pray FOR WISDOM

**Blessed be the name of God forever and ever, to whom belong wisdom and might"
(Daniel 2:20)**

PRAY FOR A DEEPER UNDERSTANDING OF WHO YOU ARE IN CHRIST + ASK GOD TO FURTHER ALIGN YOUR PURPOSE.....

I am more than a conqueror through Him who loves me (Romans 8:37).

Prayer Prompts for
Praise

- **Holiness**
- **Mercy**
- **Faithfulness**
- **Patience**
- **Holy Spirit**
- **Forgiveness**
- **Love**
- **Savior Deliverer**
- **Heavenly Father**
- **Friend**
- **Counselor**
- **Healer Provider**
- **Peace Comforter**
- **Blood**
- **Power**
- **Hope**

WRITE YOUR OWN IN THE SPACE TO THE RIGHT

Prayer Prompts for *Your Self*

- Wisdom
- As a wife or future wife
- As a mother or Future mother
- Words
- Thoughts
- A consistent Prayer Life
- Bible Study
- Confession + Repentance
- Faith
- Ministry
- Health
- Relationships
- Diet
- Exercise
- Obedience to the will of God.
- Against Temptation
- Over your Finances

WRITE YOUR OWN IN THE SPACE TO THE RIGHT

Prayer Prompts for
The World

- **The President**
- **America**
- **Governors**
- **Presidential Advisors**
- **Local Government**
- **Supreme Court**
- **Public Schools**
- **Media**
- **Military**
- **House + Senate**
- **Enemies**
- **Missionaries**
- **Economy**
- **Jerusalem**
- **Poor and Defensive People**
- **Elderly People**
- **Against Abuse**
- **Crime + Terriorism**
- **Other Religions**
- **Body of Christ**

WRITE YOUR OWN IN THE SPACE TO THE RIGHT

Prayer Prompts for
Your Children

- **Future Spouse**
- **Relationship with siblings**
- **Respect for Authority**
- **Relationship with God**
- **Obedience**
- **Will of God**
- **Purity**
- **Self Control**
- **School**
- **Heart**
- **Thoughts**
- **Words Protection**
- **Health**
- **Gifts + Calling**
- **Repentance**
- **Friends**
- **Wisdom**
- **Forgiveness**

WRITE YOUR OWN IN THE SPACE TO THE RIGHT

Prayer Prompts for
Your Husband

- **Future Spouse**
- **Priorities**
- **Daily Devotions**
- **As a Godly Husband**
- **As a Godly Father**
- **Work**
- **Finances**
- **Personal Relationship with God**
- **Health**
- **Humility**
- **Protection**
- **Integrity**
- **Thoughts**
- **Words**
- **As a leader**
- **Self Control**
- **Wisdom**
- **Peace**
- **Love**

WRITE YOUR OWN IN THE SPACE TO THE RIGHT

Prayer Requests

DATE　　　　**PRAYER REQUEST**　　　　**ANSWERED PRAYER**

Prayer Requests

DATE **PRAYER REQUEST** **ANSWERED PRAYER**

Prayer Requests

DATE **PRAYER REQUEST** **ANSWERED PRAYER**

Prayer Requests

DATE **PRAYER REQUEST** **ANSWERED PRAYER**

Prayer Requests

DATE **PRAYER REQUEST** **ANSWERED PRAYER**

Prayer Requests

DATE **PRAYER REQUEST** **ANSWERED PRAYER**

Prayer Requests

DATE   **PRAYER REQUEST**   **ANSWERED PRAYER**

Prayer Requests

DATE   **PRAYER REQUEST**   **ANSWERED PRAYER**

Prayer Requests

DATE   **PRAYER REQUEST**   **ANSWERED PRAYER**

Prayer Requests

DATE **PRAYER REQUEST** **ANSWERED PRAYER**

Prayer Requests

DATE **PRAYER REQUEST** **ANSWERED PRAYER**

DATE

Journal

SUBJECT _____

SCRIPTURE REFERENCE _____

DATE

Journal

SUBJECT _____

SCRIPTURE REFERENCE _____

DATE

Journal

SUBJECT _____

SCRIPTURE REFERENCE _____

DATE

Journal

SUBJECT_____

SCRIPTURE REFERENCE_____

DATE

Journal

SUBJECT _____

SCRIPTURE REFERENCE _____

DATE

Journal

SUBJECT _____

SCRIPTURE REFERENCE _____

DATE

Journal

SUBJECT _____

SCRIPTURE REFERENCE _____

DATE

Journal

SUBJECT _____

SCRIPTURE REFERENCE _____

DATE

Journal

SUBJECT _____

SCRIPTURE REFERENCE _____

DATE

Journal

SUBJECT _____

SCRIPTURE REFERENCE _____

DATE

Journal

SUBJECT _____

SCRIPTURE REFERENCE _____

DATE

Journal

SUBJECT _____

SCRIPTURE REFERENCE _____

DATE

Journal

SUBJECT _____

SCRIPTURE REFERENCE _____

DATE

Journal

SUBJECT _____

SCRIPTURE REFERENCE _____

DATE

Journal

SUBJECT _____

SCRIPTURE REFERENCE _____

DATE

Journal

SUBJECT _____

SCRIPTURE REFERENCE _____

DATE

Journal

SUBJECT _____

SCRIPTURE REFERENCE _____

DATE

Journal

SUBJECT _____

SCRIPTURE REFERENCE _____

DATE

Journal

SUBJECT _____

SCRIPTURE REFERENCE _____

DATE

Journal

SUBJECT _____

SCRIPTURE REFERENCE _____

DATE

Journal

SUBJECT _____

SCRIPTURE REFERENCE _____

DATE

Journal

SUBJECT _____

SCRIPTURE REFERENCE _____

DATE

Journal

SUBJECT _____

SCRIPTURE REFERENCE _____

DATE

Journal

SUBJECT _____

SCRIPTURE REFERENCE _____

DATE

Journal

SUBJECT _____

SCRIPTURE REFERENCE _____

DATE

Journal

SUBJECT _____

SCRIPTURE REFERENCE _____

DATE

Journal

SUBJECT _____

SCRIPTURE REFERENCE _____

DATE

Journal

SUBJECT _____

SCRIPTURE REFERENCE _____

DATE

Journal

SUBJECT _____

SCRIPTURE REFERENCE _____

DATE

Journal

SUBJECT _____

SCRIPTURE REFERENCE _____

DATE

Journal

SUBJECT _____

SCRIPTURE REFERENCE _____

Made in the USA
Monee, IL
25 July 2020